796.32
M

8554

May, Julian
The NBA playoffs

SPORTS CLASSIC

THE
N.B.A. PLAYOFFS
BASKEBALLS CLASSIC

By JULIAN MAY

Creative Education
Mankato, Minnesota

Photograph and Illustration Credits

ILLUSTRATORS

John Keely, Minneapolis 11, 18, 20, 42

PHOTOGRAPHERS

Vernon J. Biever, Green Bay, Wisconsin 2, 10-11, 29, 31, 34, 36, 39, 42, 44, 46
UPI 1, 8, 13, 14, 16, 19, 21, 27, 32, 40
Sheedy & Long, Inc. 23

Published by Creative Educational Society, Inc., 123 South Broad Street,
Mankato, Minnesota 56001. Copyright © 1975 by Creative Educational
Society, Inc. International copyrights reserved in all countries.
No part of this book may be reproduced in any form without written
permission from the publisher. Printed in the United States.
Distributed by Childrens Press, 1224 West Van Buren Street, Chicago,
Illinois 60607.
Library of Congress Number: 75-17755   ISBN: 0-87191-448-4
Library of Congress Cataloging in Publication Data
May, Julian.   The NBA playoffs.
   (Sports classic)
   SUMMARY: A brief history of the National Basketball
Association playoff games.
   1. National Basketball Association—Juvenile literature.
2. Basketball—Juvenile literature.
(1. National Basketball Association.   2. Basketball)   I. Title.
GB885.515.N37M39 796.32'364'0973 75-17755 ISBN 0-87191-448-4

Contents

7 Birth Of The NBA
10 The First Great Play-off
17 The Clutch Masters
21 Wilt and The Champs
24 Comeback For The Celtics
26 Sic 'Em, Knicks!
30 The Instant Dynasty
33 At Long Last, Lakers
38 Cap'n Willis Returns
41 The Sweetest Title Of All
47 NBA Champion Teams

Birth Of The NBA

They called them "the bad old days."

Of all pro sports, basketball had the hardest time being born. College and high-school basketball became very popular with sports fans. But not the pro game. There were no arenas where large crowds could watch the game. So the early pro teams had a hard time making money. Teams and small leagues would spring up, live for awhile, then die.

In the late 1930's, the Midwest had a struggling pro circuit called the National Basketball League. After World War II, this league began to do well. People were eager for winter-time sports fun.

A group of businessmen who owned hockey arenas in the East looked at basketball with new interest. They decided to form a league of their own — the Basketball Association of America. The BAA began to play in 1946. It prospered. Within two years, it swallowed up the older NBL.

The present-day National Basketball Association was formed from the two leagues in 1949.

The first pro basketball superstar was George Mikan of the Minneapolis Lakers. His team had been part of the old NBL. After the merger, Mikan and his Lakers won the first NBA championship.

The other great star of early pro basketball was Joe Fulks. He started with the BAA Philadelphia Warriors in 1946 and helped them win the championship. Fulks was the new league's top scorer.

In those early days, basketball scores were not very high. Fulks astonished fans by scoring 63 points

on February 10, 1949. It was more than many a team could rack up. When Fulks retired in 1954, he had amassed a total of 8,003 points, second only to George Mikan's total of 11,764.

In its early years, the NBA had a "color barrier" that prevented black players from joining the teams. But times were changing. The talent of black athletes could no longer be ignored once Jackie Robinson integrated baseball in the mid-1940's. The Harlem Globetrotters basketball team played to packed houses all over the country. If white fans weren't afraid to cheer the Globetrotters, why wouldn't they cheer black players in the NBA?

In 1950, the first black player was drafted from college. He was Chuck Cooper, who went to the Boston Celtics. After him many other black players were hired.

Pro basketball had a crisis in the early 1950's. Fans were getting bored because the game was slowing down. Players stalled and fouled too much.

In order to save the pro game, the rules were changed to speed up play. The most important new rule was the "24 seconds to shoot" rule. This rule gave basketball its modern, exciting image. It turned the sport from a small-time into a big-time game.

Tom Heinsohn (15) was the highest-scoring forward of the champion Boston Celtics during the late 1950's and early 1960's. In 1969, he became coach of the team and rebuilt it to greatness. Here he goes for a basket with a hook shot over the arm of Vern Mikkelsen of the Minneapolis Lakers in 1959.

The First Great Play-off

Crowds at modern basketball games testify to the game's popularity. But in the beginning, it wasn't necessarily so!

For their first four seasons, the Boston Celtics were hopeless losers. By 1950, owner Walter Brown had lost nearly all the money he had invested in the team. He was at the end of his rope.

Then two miracles saved him and the team. The first was a crusty new coach named Arnold (Red) Auerbach. The second was a little bitty backcourt man named Bob Cousy.

Coach Auerbach sneered when Brown drew Cousy's name out of a hat at the college draft. Cousy was only 6-foot-1! What good was a shrimp to the Celtics?

A lot of good. The little man could do magical things with a basketball. He palmed and faked and even dribbled behind his back! Fans loved his antics. And they paid good money to watch him.

Coach Auerbach brought the team in second during his rookie season. And Boston was on its way to glory. In 1956-57, the Celtics acquired two players that would complete the miracle begun in 1950. The first was Tom Heinsohn. The second was Bill Russell. These outstanding new men helped the team to a first-place slot in the Eastern Division.

That year, the play-off finals attracted national attention for the first time. It was Boston vs St. Louis. The first game went to St. Louis in overtime, 125-123. The second was Boston's, 119-99.

Bob Cousy (14), the "Mighty Midget," was famed for his flashy behavior on court. Here he palms the ball to teammate Tom Heinsohn (15), who then scored on a lay-up. The action came during the second game of the final play-offs of 1957.

Then St. Louis won the third game at home, but blew the chance to wrap up the series when Boston bounced back and won the fourth game and the fifth.

It looked like the end for the Hawks. But in the sixth game, with the score tied and *one second* to go, Cliff Hagan of St. Louis scored and won the game. The series was tied up, 3-3.

The seventh and deciding game was played in Boston on April 13, 1957. The entire United States seemed to be holding its breath over a pro basketball game for the first time in history.

The last game was full of suspense. With seconds remaining, St. Louis led. Then a free throw by Cousy made it 103-101. St. Louis's star, Bob Pettit, sank two free throws and pushed the game into overtime.

At the end of the first overtime period, the score was tied again at 113-113. A second overtime period began. This time, the Hawks were down, 125-123, with two seconds to play. They tried one last play. Alex Hannum threw and hit. Pettit got the rebound and tried to score. . . .

The ball hit the rim. The buzzer sounded. And the Boston Celtics were NBA champions for the first time.

The first MVP award in the NBA was given in 1956 to Bob Pettit (9) of the St. Louis Hawks. He was a great scorer who became the first in the league to rack up 20,000 points. Under the old rules, such a total would have been impossible. Pettit played from 1954 until 1965, winning a second MVP in 1959.

The Clutch Masters

In 1958, Boston finished the regular season as top team in the NBA. For the second time, they met St. Louis in the finals and were favored to win. But Bill Russell sprained his ankle in the third game — and Boston went down the drain, 4 games to 2.

However, after that, everything would come up shamrocks for the Celtics. They embarked on the most amazing winning streak in the history of sports. For the next eight years, Coach Red Auerbach skippered the NBA champions. And in all but the last of those years, the Celtics led the NBA in won-lost percentage, too.

Many times, they seemed doomed to defeat — only to prove themselves masters in the clutch. In the 1962 semifinal play-off, they were up against the Philadelphia Warriors. Philly's giant star, Wilt Chamberlain, had averaged an awesome 50.4 points per game that year. The teams fought through seven games and were tied, 107-107, in the last 16 seconds. Boston's bacon was saved by the Jones Boys, K.C. and Sam, who worked together and scored.

In the finals against the Lakers, the Celtics came to the clutch again — the score was tied, 100-100, in the last 5 seconds of the seventh game! Los

In the 1963 play-offs, Celtic K.C. Jones (25) and Gene Wiley (12) of the Lakers take to the air after a wild ball. Bill Russell (6) watches in the background — while Frank Ramsey (23) and Rudy LaRusso (35) hold their breath.

Angeles got the ball, but its shot rolled off the rim of the basket. In the overtime, Boston led, 110-107, with 22 seconds left. Cousy dribbled out the clock, and the Celtics were champs for the fourth time in a row.

In 1963, Oscar Robertson of the Cincinnati Royals gave Boston a tough time in the semifinals. But the Celtics conquered, 4 games to 3. Then they tramped over the Lakers to win the title, 4 games to 2.

Bob Cousy retired after 13 glittering years. Some people thought this spelled the end of the Boston dynasty. How could the Celtics stay on top without their little ball-handling wizard of offense?

Coach Red Auerbach showed his genius by changing Boston's strategy. The team leaned more heavily on a defensive style. Anchored by Bill Russell, the defensive marvel, the new game panned out so well that the team did even better in 1964 than it had in 1963!

The Celtics put away Cincinnati again in the semis. Their foe in the finals was San Francisco (formerly the Philadelphia Warriors). Once again it was Russell against Chamberlain, who had earned his fifth straight scoring title. The two big men had become basketball's greatest rivals — Mr. Defense *vs.* Mr. Offense. In 1964, it was Russell and the Celtics who won. Poor Wilt the Stilt played well — but the rest of his team couldn't cut the mustard. Boston won the title, 4 games to 1.

In the 1966 finals, Bill Russell goes up for a shot at the hoop, only to find Los Angeles Laker LeRoy Ellis there, blocking the shot. Jerry West darts across in front.

The next season, a new team sprang up in Philadelphia — the 76ers. In mid-season, they acquired Wilt Chamberlain in a stunning trade. The 76ers almost downed Boston in the semis that year. But once again the Celtics won in the clutch. In the last 5 seconds of the seventh game, Havlicek intercepted a Philly pass to save Boston's 110-109 squeaker victory.

The 1965 final against Los Angeles was an anticlimax. Boston won, 4 games to 1.

In 1966, Coach Auerbach's last season, Boston and LA met in the finals again. But this series proved to be anything but a Boston laugher.

To Auerbach's dismay, the Celtics dropped the first game, 133-129. Hoping to rally his men, the coach announced his selection for next season's skipper: none other than Bill Russell!

The happy Celtics won the next three games in a row. But the Lakers weren't dead yet. They won two games and evened the series. The seventh game was a heart-pounder. Russell got 32 rebounds and 25 points. In the end, the Celtics mastered another clutch situation. They won, 95-93.

It was their eighth straight NBA title.

Wilt Chamberlain of the Philadelphia 76ers was a basketball Goliath who combined size, strength, and agility. His independent mind made him nearly impossible to coach, however. For most of his career, he tended to be a one-man team until his later years with the Lakers. He was the first man to score more than 3,000 points in a season (1960-61).

Wilt and The Champs

He was the tallest, the strongest, the top scorer for seven seasons in a row, the top rebounder of the year, the man who had never fouled out, the year's Most Valuable Player.

And they called him a loser.

He was Wilt Chamberlain at the end of the 1965-66 season. Troubled, brooding, "impossible to coach," he was so good that he had overbalanced the San Francisco Warriors (formerly of Philadelphia). So they traded him back East to the Philadelphia 76ers (formerly the Syracuse Nationals).

And his team, as always, had lost the play-offs.

But the next season, Philadelphia was finally able to dial the winning combination. The team got a new coach, Alex Hannum, who was really Chamberlain's *old* coach from San Francisco and Philly! Hannum tightened up the men he had and acquired new strength for the backcourt.

The result was a team that won 45 of their first 49 games. Wilt Chamberlain no longer had to be a one-man team. He lost his scoring title that year — but his team won 68 games and lost only 13 — an incredible average of .840!

In the semifinals, the 76ers rolled over Bill Russell's Celtics, 4 games to 1. The Celts were aging, and Coach Russell hadn't yet learned how to rebuild.

Then came the finals. It was Philly vs. San Francisco.

The Warriors put up a tough fight in game one. But Philadelphia won, 141-135, in overtime. The next contest was an easy Philly victory. Then the series traveled to the West Coast, and San Francisco won at home, 130-124.

22

Bill Russell (6) and Elgin Baylor contend for the ball in the 1968 NBA play-offs.

The 76ers took game four, and the Warriors won the next one. In the sixth game, Wilt Chamberlain played a remarkable *defensive* game. He checked the Warriors' Rick Barry, league-leading scorer, so that he missed a crucial basket in the last seconds of the game.

With the score 123-122, Philadelphia kept its slender lead and even added 2 more points on a foul. They won the game and the NBA title.

And happy Wilt Chamberlain knew that nobody could call him a "loser" any more.

Comeback For The Celtics

When Bill Russell took over the helm of the Celtics in 1966, he became the first black man to coach a major-league team — in any sport.

And he had a tough row to hoe.

Any new coach has a hard time breaking in. Bill Russell had some extra problems. The race thing wasn't so bad. The real trouble was, the Celtics were a gang of "old men." Many key players were over 30. Bill himself, the player-coach, was 32. In basketball, one of the most grueling of sports, it helps if you are young. It helps a lot.

During Bill Russell's first season as coach, the Celtics came in second in their division. They were defeated in the semis by Philadelphia. Boston fans sadly believed that the dynasty was over.

But they were reckoning without Bill Russell. Born in Louisiana and raised in California, he became a 6-foot-9-inch sensation on the basketball team of the University of San Francisco. The team won 56 straight games. Bill was twice All-American.

When he came to the Celtics in the middle of the 1956-57 season, he proved to be the magic charm that won Boston their first title. As a center, he led the league in rebounding four times. His specialty was grabbing high passes, leaping into the air, and pushing the ball through the hoop.

Keenly intelligent and sensitive, he won the deep respect of his team. Sportswriters and fans did not always appreciate him. He was too outspoken. He didn't care whose toes he stepped on as long as he did the best possible job on the court.

In Russell's second year as coach, 1967-68, the "tired old men" once again came in second in the Eastern Division. But this time they beat Philly in the semifinals, 4 games to 3. And they won their tenth NBA title by taking Los Angeles, 4 to 2.

Was it just a fluke? Next season, poor old Boston was fourth in the East. But they destroyed Philly in the first round, 4 to 1. In the semis, they whipped New York in 6 games. Los Angeles, now starring Wilt Chamberlain, was a 2-to-1 favorite in the finals.

But Boston beat them in 7 tough games. Then, at age 35, Bill Russell retired. He had proved his point.

Sic 'Em, Knicks!

During the days of the great coach, Joe Lapchick, the New York Knicks had been tops in the East. But that was in the early 1950's. The team fell on hard times indeed after Lapchick left. They went to the cellar in 1956. And except for a brief surge in 1959, they stayed at the bottom for the next ten years.

Then they got lucky in the draft. In the 60's, they got Willis Reed, Butch Komives, Bill Bradley, Walt Frazier, and several other good hands. But even with this talent, Coach Dick McGuire couldn't make the Knicks last past the first round of the play-offs. In 1968, the team started to slide toward last place again.

The Knicks fired McGuire and hired Red Holzman. Finally, the gears started to mesh. The team was third in the East, the best they had done in ten years.

Next season, they were third again — and made it to the semifinals. In 1969-70, they were first in the league at last! Reed and Frazier were rated among the top players in the NBA.

Joe Lapchick was pro basketball's Grand Old Man. A member of Basketball's Hall of Fame, he was star center for the Original Celtics during the 1920's and '30's, when the team was best in the world. Lapchick coached the New York Knicks from 1947 until 1956, and also coached an outstanding series of college teams at St. John's University. His basketball career spanned 50 years.

That season's play-offs were the most exciting in years. In the first round, New York defeated Baltimore, 4 games to 3. In the semis, the Knicks met Milwaukee — which boasted young superstar Lew Alcindor, Rookie of the Year. New York prevailed easily, 4 games to 1.

Then came the wild final. The Knicks' opponent was Los Angeles, making its seventh try for the championship in nine years.

The Knicks were good because of their balance. Coach Holzman had crafted a pressing defense, and an offense that operated like a Swiss watch. All of the players worked. They didn't have to depend on one or two superstars.

New York and Los Angeles split the first four games. In the fifth, Knick Willis Reed, the league MVP, tore a muscle. The Knicks won the fifth anyhow, but they dropped the next game with Reed on the bench.

In the decider, Reed was back on the floor, playing in spite of the pain. He hardly scored, but he did check Chamberlain. Meanwhile, Walt Frazier got 36 points and 19 assists!

Clearly superior, the Knicks won, 113-99, and took their first NBA title.

28

Walt Frazier of the New York Knicks shows his famous dribble. He electrified the basketball world with his ball-hawking.

The Instant Dynasty

As pro basketball gained in favor with the fans, the NBA expanded. A new team named the Bucks started in Milwaukee in 1968-69. It finished at the bottom of the division. This happy disaster gave Milwaukee the right to draft the most promising rookie since Wilt Chamberlain was a pup.

His name was Lew Alcindor. He was a 7-foot-1 wonder from UCLA, winner of the first Naismith Award as top college basketball player.

In his first season, the young giant helped hoist the Bucks to second place. Alcindor was an overwhelming choice for Rookie of the Year.

Next season, the Bucks hired veteran Oscar Robertson from the Cincinnati Royals, He ranked third among lifetime scorers. Many thought he was over the hill. But Milwaukee Coach Larry Costello managed to blend the talents of Alcindor and Robertson to create what the happy Milwaukee fans called an "instant dynasty."

The Bucks took first place in 1970-71, winning 66 games and losing only 16. They downed San Francisco in the first play-off round, 4 to 1. Then they rolled the Lakers in 5 games, too.

Their rival for the title was Baltimore — another "Cinderella" team. The Bullets had made the finals largely because Willis Reed of the Knicks had been

Oscar Robertson, the Big O, has been recognized as one of the greatest guards of all time. He played first for Cincinnati, then joined the Milwaukee Bucks in 1970. Without his experience it is doubtful that Bucks could have come so far, so fast.

injured, giving Baltimore a narrow victory in the semis.

In the finals, mighty Milwaukee did just what the world expected. The Bucks destroyed the Bullets, 4 games in a row. The Instant Dynasty couldn't lose!

At Long Last, Lakers

They were born in Minneapolis in 1947, part of the old National Basketball League. Their great star was George Mikan. The next season, the team jumped to the BAA and became champions. The Lakers won the title five times in the early years of the BAA (later, the NBA). But after Mikan retired, the team went downhill. The franchise moved to Los Angeles in 1960.

The team had one great star — a young player named Elgin Baylor. And it had a promising rookie — a short but high-scoring Olympic champion named Jerry West.

In their second season, the Los Angeles Lakers were division champs. They were destined to become one of the great basketball teams of the NBA. Seven times in eleven years, they reached the play-offs and needed to win just one more game to reach the championship.

And seven times, they failed.

Jerry West became one of basketball's superstars. Wilt Chamberlain joined the Lakers in 1968. The team topped their division five times. But the NBA title kept slipping away.

Watching the bouncing ball during the 1970 title series are *(left to right)* Willis Reed, Elgin Baylor, Wilt Chamberlain, and Dave Debusschere.

33

In 1971-72, the Lakers had their greatest season. They won 69 games and only lost 13 — a new record. Surely this was the year for the championship!

The first play-off round was against Chicago. Los Angeles swept it in four games. Then came their toughest opponent, the defending champion Milwaukee Bucks. It was Jerry West *vs.* Oscar Robertson, and Wilt Chamberlain *vs.* Kareem Abdul-Jabbar (formerly Lew Alcindor).

The Lakers got slaughtered, 93-72.

In the second game, the Lakers won a squeaker, 135-134. The hero of the game was young Jim McMillian, who scored a career high of 42 points.

Game No. 3 was a virtual contest between Chamberlain and Kareem Abdul-Jabbar. Milwaukee

Wilt Chamberlain and Jim McMillian (5) battle
the Milwaukee Bucks in the 1972 play-offs.

led, 99-95, in the last 4 minutes. But Jerry West, McMillian, and the defensive talents of Chamberlain pulled it out. Los Angeles won its second victory, 108-105.

Milwaukee routed the Lakers in the fourth game, 114-88, to even the series. Laker Coach Bill Sharman was very worried. His team had won twice — narrowly. They had lost twice — by a whopping margin.

But the next game was played in California. The hungry, loyal fans cheered the Lakers to a third win. Returning to Milwaukee, the Bucks faced sudden death.

And they died. The Lakers won the semis in 6.

Now came the finals, against the Knicks. Their star center, Willis Reed, was out with injuries. But New York was no pushover. The Knicks won the first game, 114-92. Then it was the Lakers' turn for a crusher. They won the second one, 106-92. When the series moved to New York, the Lakers continued to dominate. They won games No. 3 and 4.

One more game would do it! It was played at Los Angeles. Wilt Chamberlain had a sprained wrist. But he refused to sit out the crucial game. He proved to be the driving force as the Lakers won, 114-100, to become NBA champions at last.

Jerry West of the Los Angeles Lakers has been nicknamed "Mr. Clutch" because of his out-standing performance in tight situations. Only 6-feet-3 and 175 pounds, he played his 12th season for LA in 1971-72.

Cap'n Willis Returns

Willis Reed seemed to have reached his peak in 1970. After a brilliant season, he saw his team go into the finals looking like champions.

But in the fifth game, Reed pulled a leg muscle. The next contest saw him on the bench while the Lakers made hay. Wilt Chamberlain, with no Willis Reed to guard him, led LA to its third victory and evened the series.

Captain Willis said of the crucial seventh game: "I'll play if I have to crawl."

He played. And the Knicks won the title.

In the following season, Willis Reed played in spite of an injured knee. He had an operation, but the injury got worse. He played in only 11 games in the 1971-72 season. Some people said he was finished.

Reed would not give up. He was back in uniform the next season. But at first, he was as inept as a rookie. He couldn't run or shoot. He lacked confidence.

Slowly, Cap'n Willis came back. All it cost was time and pain. He led the Knicks as they clobbered Baltimore in the play-offs, 4 games to 1. Then the team licked the powerful Celtics in 7 tough games.

For the finals, the Knicks met Los Angeles. The Lakers won the first game, but New York — led by Reed — took the next four in a row. It was

Willis Reed, captain of the New York Knicks, was named Most Valuable Player of both the 1970 and 1973 play-off series — years in which the team was NBA champion. He stands 6-feet-10 and weighs 245 pounds. Reed had played with the Knicks since 1964.

a reversal of the 1972 play-offs, and Willis Reed was MVP.

He said: "It was really a team effort. They should cut up the MVP award and give a piece to everyone who contributed."

The Sweetest Title Of All

The dynasty was dead. Everyone said so.

The Boston Celtics had won their last NBA title in 1969 under Bill Russell. His postion as team leader had been inherited by John Havlicek. His coaching mantle had fallen on Tom Heinsohn, another old Boston player from the Golden Age.

But neither man had been able to carry on the winning tradition. At least, not at the start. Painful years of rebuilding had to come first — and a great rookie named Dave Cowens!

Cowens, a 6-foot-8½ center, was drafted in 1970. A lot of people said he was too small for the middle. But Cowens made up in speed and hustle what he lacked in size. In his first season, Dave helped Boston back to a winning record. He was named Rookie of the Year.

The Celtics kept on improving. In 1973, they nearly beat out the Knicks in the semis.

Next season, 1973-74, they stopped Buffalo neatly in the first round. Then they polished off the Knicks in the semifinals, 4 games to 1.

In the finals, it was Celtics *vs.* Bucks. Milwau-

Wilt Chamberlain tries to block a throw by Willis Reed (19) in the third game of the 1970 play-off finals.

kee's Kareem Abdul-Jabbar was easily the game's No. 1 center. But Cowens was ranked second. Milwaukee had a great scorer in Bob Dandridge. But the rest of their team lacked zing. Oscar Robertson, once a superstar, was in the twilight of a great career, ready to retire.

The Celtics entered the last round of the play-offs full of confidence. But it wasn't to be a waltz. Boston and Milwaukee split the first four games.

In the fifth game, Boston pulled ahead. The sixth game was to be one of the most exciting in years.

The Bucks managed to contain Cowens during most of the contest. But with a minute left, Dave came through in the clutch with a long one that tied the score, 86-86, and forced the game into overtime.

The first overtime period ended when Boston's John Havlicek got a rebound off his own miss. The second overtime saw Havlicek roll up 9 points. Boston seemed to have it sewed up.

But in last 4 seconds, Kareem coolly hooked the ball 18 feet and won it for Milwaukee, 102-101.

So the series went to a seventh game. The Bucks zeroed in on Havlicek — who would be named MVP of the play-offs. Coach Heinsohn had planned a new strategy to outwit the Bucks.

It featured Dave Cowens. While the Bucks clamped down on Havlicek, holding him to 16 points, Cowens went romping around, setting up his teammates out of the reach of the towering Abdul-Jabbar.

The Celtics built up a halftime lead of 53-40 before Milwaukee realized what was happening and tightened its defense.

In the fourth period, Boston's lead was shortened. But the Bucks continued to stick close to Havlicek, while Dave Cowens and the other Celtics were able to score.

In the last quarter, Boston scored eight points in a row. The Bucks tightened up. They eased their watch on Havlicek — only to have him clinch the victory with a 3-point play down the middle! The Celtics won, 102-87.

John Havlicek said: "This team has a lot of pride. The younger guys got tired of hearing how great the old Celtics were. They went out and proved that they have championship quality themselves."

The old champ was dead, long live the new! It had to happen in sports' fastest moving game, in the NBA play-offs.

Dave Cowens of Newport, Kentucky, went to Florida State, where he starred but attracted little attention. All of that changed when he joined the Celtics. He was named MVP in 1972-73. Here he eyes the ball as it soars toward the basket during the 1974 finals. Cornell Warner of the Bucks hovers behind him.

NBA Champion Teams

1946-47	Philadelphia
1947-48	Baltimore
1948-49	Minneapolis
1949-50	Minneapolis
1950-51	Rochester
1951-52	Minneapolis
1952-53	Minneapolis
1953-54	Minneapolis
1954-55	Syracuse
1955-56	Philadelphia
1956-57	Boston
1957-58	St. Louis
1958-59	Boston
1959-60	Boston
1960-61	Boston
1961-62	Boston
1962-63	Boston
1963-64	Boston
1964-65	Boston
1965-66	Boston
1966-67	Philadelphia
1967-68	Boston
1968-69	Boston
1969-70	New York
1970-71	Milwaukee
1971-72	Los Angeles
1972-73	New York
1973-74	Boston

The 1949-50 season was the first in which NBA teams played. Prior to this, the NBA was known as the Basketball Association of America. It merged with the National Basketball League in 1949 to form the NBA.

John Havlicek of the Boston Celtics links the modern glory days of Boston with old dynasty of Bill Russell, Bob Cousy, and the Greatest Team Ever. Havlicek began his pro career with the Celtics in 1962. He stands 6-feet-5 and weighs 205 pounds. He is Boston's all-time scoring champion. Trying to stop Havlicek in the 1974 finals is Milwaukee's Bob Dandridge.

47

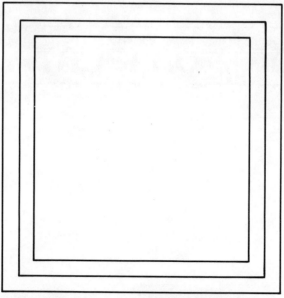

SPORTS CLASSICS

WORLD SERIES
U.S. OPEN GOLF CHAMPIONSHIP
WIMBLEDON TENNIS TOURNAMENT
KENTUCKY DERBY
INDIANAPOLIS 500
OLYMPIC GAMES
SUPER BOWL
MASTERS TOURNAMENT OF GOLF
STANLEY CUP
NBA PLAYOFFS

CREATIVE EDUCATION